The
SUMMER OLYMPICS
ON THE WORLD STAGE

RECORD
BREAKERS

The SUMMER OLYMPICS
ON THE WORLD STAGE

ATHLETES TO WATCH

FASCINATING FACTS

GREATEST MOMENTS

RECORD BREAKERS

The SUMMER OLYMPICS
ON THE WORLD STAGE

RECORD BREAKERS

SCOTT MCDONALD

MASON CREST
PHILADELPHIA | MIAMI

MASON CREST
450 Parkway Drive, Suite D, Broomall, Pennsylvania 19008
(866) MCP-BOOK (toll-free) • www.masoncrest.com

Printed and bound in the United States of America.

First printing

9 8 7 6 5 4 3 2 1
ISBN (hardback) 978-1-4222-4447-0
ISBN (series) 978-1-4222-4443-2
ISBN (ebook) 978-1-4222-7368-5

Library of Congress Cataloging-in-Publication Data

Names: McDonald, Scott (Sports journalist), author. | Mason Crest Publishers.
Title: Record breakers / Scott McDonald.
Description: Broomall, Pennsylvania : Mason Crest, 2020. | Series: The Summer
    Olympics: On the world stage | Includes bibliographical references and index.
Identifiers: LCCN 2019042176 | ISBN 9781422244470 (Hardback) | ISBN
    9781422273685 (eBook) | ISBN 9781422244432 (Series)
Subjects: LCSH: Olympic athletes–Juvenile literature. | Olympics–History–Juvenile
    literature. | Olympic Games–History–Juvenile literature.
Classification: LCC GV721.53 .M35 2020 | DDC 796.48–dc23
LC record available at https://lccn.loc.gov/2019042176

Developed and Produced by National Highlights Inc.
Editor: Andrew Luke
Production: Crafted Content LLC

Cover images, clockwise from top left:

American swimmer Michael Phelps (Fernando Frazao Agencia Brasil@Wikimedia Commons), Medal ceremony for swimmers at the Beijing 2002 Summer Games (Jmex60@Wikimedia Commons), Jamaican sprinter Usain Bolt (Jmex60@Wikimedia Commons), Romanian Gymnast Nadia Comăneci (Public domain@Wikimedia Commons)

QR CODES AND LINKS TO THIRD-PARTY CONTENT

CONTENTS

WHAT ARE THE SUMMER OLYMPICS?

The ancient Olympic Games took place in Greece every four years for nearly 12 centuries from 776 BC through 393 AD. They were part of a religious festival to honor Zeus, who was the father of Greek gods and goddesses. The event was held in Olympia, a sanctuary site named for Mount Olympus, which is the country's tallest mountain and the mythological home of the Greek gods. It is the place for which the Olympics are named.

Roughly 1,500 years after the ancient Games ended, a Frenchman named Baron Pierre de Coubertin wanted to resurrect the Olympic Games to coincide with the 1900 World Fair in Paris. The 1900 Paris Exposition was to feature the newest, modern-day, turn-of-the-century attractions like talking films, the diesel engine, escalators, magnet audio recorders, and a fairly new Eiffel Tower painted yellow.

De Coubertin wanted the best athletes in the world for the first modern Olympic Games outside of Greece, so he presented the idea in 1894. Representatives from 34 potential countries got so excited about his plan that they proposed the Games take place in 1896 instead. So, the modern Olympics, as it is now called, began where the ancient Games left off—in Athens, Greece, in 1896.

The 10-day event in April 1896 had 241 male athletes from 14 countries competing in 43 events. The events at these Athens Games were athletics (track and field), swimming, cycling, fencing, gymnastics, shooting, tennis, weightlifting, and wrestling. The ancient Games had consisted of short races, days-long boxing matches, and chariot races.

Like the ancient Games, organizers held the event every four years, with Paris hosting in 1900, when women made their first appearance. The Paris Games had many more competitors, as 997 athletes represented 24 countries in 95 total events. These Games were spread out from May through October to coincide with the Paris Exposition.

The Summer Olympics have now spanned into the 21st century and have become the ultimate crowning achievement for athletes worldwide. The Games have evolved with the addition and removal of events, the scope of media coverage, the addition of a separate Winter Olympics, and the emergence of both the Special Olympics and Paralympic Games.

The Olympics have been the site of great athletic feats and sportsmanship. They have presented tragedy, triumph, controversy, and political grandstanding. There have been legendary athletes, remarkable human-interest stories, doping allegations, boycotts, terrorist attacks, and three cancellations because of worldwide war.

Yet the Olympics, with its five interlocking rings and eternal flame, remain a symbol of unity and hope.

The United States hosted its first Games in 1904 in St. Louis, Missouri, which, like Paris, spread the Games over several months in conjunction with the World Fair. The presentation of gold, silver, and bronze medals for finishing first, second, and third in each event began at this Olympics.

More than 2,000 athletes competed in England at the 1908 London Games, which were originally scheduled for Rome but reassigned once organizers discovered the Italian capital would not be ready in time. In London, the marathon race was extended by 195 meters so the finish line would be just below the royal box in the stadium and thus the 26.2 miles from the 1908 edition went on to become the official marathon distance beginning with the 1924 Paris Games.

Stockholm, Sweden, hosted the 1912 Games, and the Olympics were cancelled in 1916 because of World War I (WWI). Other years in which the Olympic Games were not held include 1940 and 1944 because of World War II.

Berlin, Germany, had been awarded the 1916 Olympics that were cancelled, but rather than reward the Germans following WWI by giving them the 1920 Games, they were instead awarded to Antwerp, Belgium, to honor the Belgians who suffered so many hardships during the war. The Olympic flag, which shows five interlocked rings to signify the universality of the Games, was first hoisted during the 1920 opening ceremonies in Antwerp. The Olympic rings have become a well-known symbol of sportsmanship and unity worldwide.

The 1924 Games were back in Paris, and the Olympics became a recognized, bona fide worldwide event. The number of participating countries went from 29 to 44. There were more than 3,000 athletes competing and more than 1,000 journalists covering the competition.

Also, in 1924, the annual event became known as the Summer Olympics, or Summer Games, as the Winter Olympics debuted in Chamonix, France. The Winter Games were held every four years through 1992. The Winter Olympics were then held again in 1994 and every four years since then.

Two more long-standing traditions began at the 1928 Summer Games in Amsterdam, Netherlands. The Olympic flame was lit for the first time in a cauldron at the top of the Olympic stadium. Also, during the opening ceremony, the national team of Greece entered the stadium first and the Dutch entered last, signifying the first team to host the modern Olympics and the current host. This tradition still stands today.

The United States got its second Summer Olympics in 1932, when Los Angeles, California, hosted. The city built a lavish coliseum for the Games, and it was the last time the USA would host the Summer Olympics for 52 years, when they were once again held in Los Angeles in 1984, at the same stadium.

The 1936 Summer Olympics in Berlin also produced some long-lasting, first-time traditions. These Games were the first to have a torch relay bringing the Olympic flame to the stadium, and they were also the first to be televised.

The Summer Olympics took a 12-year hiatus because of World War II, and London was once again called upon to host the Games with short notice in 1948.

The Summer Games have been held every four years since 1948. In 2016, Rio de Janeiro, Brazil, hosted the Summer Games, and that meant the Olympics had now been held on five continents. Australia has hosted the Summer Olympics twice (Melbourne in 1956 and Sydney in 2000). Asia has hosted four times (Tokyo, Japan in 1964 and 2020; Seoul, Korea, in 1988; and Beijing, China, in 2008).

Other North American cities to host the Summer Olympics have been Mexico City, Mexico, in 1968; Montreal, Canada, in 1976; and Atlanta, Georgia, in 1996 for the centennial anniversary of the modern Olympics. Los Angeles will host the Games for a third time in 2028.

Although athletes typically garner headlines for most Olympic coverage, sometimes events outside of the playing field force the world to take notice.

Eight Palestinian terrorists shot two Israeli athletes dead and held nine more as hostages during the 1972 Munich Games in Germany. Those nine were also murdered during a botched rescue attempt.

The 1980 Moscow Games in Russia saw the fewest number of athletes in a Summer Olympics since 1956, when the USA led a boycott of Moscow after the Soviet Union invaded Afghanistan in December of 1979.

The Soviet Union then led a contingency of Eastern European nations that boycotted the 1984 Los Angeles Games during the Cold War, mainly as payback for the U.S. boycott.

The first Summer Olympics that were boycott-free since 1972 were the 1992 Games in Barcelona, Spain, which was also the first time professional basketball players competed, opening the door for professionals in all Olympic sports except wrestling and boxing. Before the International Olympic Committee (IOC) approved professional athletes to participate in the late 1980s, the Olympics were primarily for the world's best amateur athletes.

Many have lamented the demise of amateurism at the Olympic Games, but by far the most contentious issue the IOC has dealt with in recent years is the scourge of steroids and other prohibited performance-enhancing drugs.

The world's greatest celebration of sport has had a checkered and colorful past, from politics and doping to sheer athleticism and the triumph of the human spirit. This century has seen the Summer Games return to familiar places (Athens 2004, London 2012) and expand to new ones (Sydney 2000, Rio de Janeiro 2016). Tokyo awaits the world in 2020, when the newest great Olympic stories will be told.

– Scott McDonald, Olympic and Paralympic Journalist

RECORD BREAKERS

The best athletes in the world train to make the Olympics every four years, and it is almost inevitable that some type of record will either be tied or broken during the games. As athletes from around the world hone their skills for the ultimate competition, records are bound to fall.

The record might be an Olympic standard that falls in one event, or it may be a number of records that get broken at any given Summer Games. American swimmer Mark Spitz won seven gold medals at the 1972 Munich Games, and American swimmer Michael Phelps won eight at the 2008 Beijing Games. Spitz retired at just twenty-two after Munich, while Phelps went to four Olympics and won 28 medals, with 23 of them gold — both records.

Sometimes an athlete can achieve something that has never been done before, or they might match one record and go on to further Olympic achievements like Carl Lewis did in four Olympic appearances.

The Olympics often see world records set that stand several years, or even decades. Some marks that are solely Olympic records have stood more than 30 years. There are teams that have broken records like U.S. women's beach volleyball and China table tennis, or individual athletes who, like Americans Wilma Rudolph in 1960 or Bob Beamon in 1968, gave memorable performances.

Some athletes, like Romanian gymnast Nadia Comaneci, achieved perfection, and others, like American Greg Louganis, got redemption after what appeared to be a crushing setback.

Usain Bolt, the Flying Finn, Jesse Owens, and Flo-Jo are all names that are also etched in Olympic history because they did things that no human had ever done before—they were record breakers.

BOB BEAMON
USA TRACK AND FIELD

World Record Long Jump at 1968 Mexico City Games

Bob Beamon didn't just set a new world record with his long jump at the 1968 Mexico City Olympics; he obliterated it. Beamon became the first human to break the 28- and 29-foot barriers, and he did it on just one jump.

During his first attempt in the final round, Beamon took off from the back of the runway, using his great speed to build momentum. Beamon leaped high into the air and soared, landing close to the back of the sand pit with his backside lightly scraping the sand.

Beamon's distance didn't automatically appear, and meet officials measured the jump manually.

"When they brought out the measuring tape, I thought I may have jumped 27 feet 10 inches," Beamon said years later during an interview. That alone would have crushed the world record of 27 feet, 4 ¾ inches.

After more than 10 minutes, his jump of 8.90 meters appeared on the scoreboard at Estadio Olímpico

LAST CHANCE QUALIFIER

History almost never happened for Beamon in the 1968 Games. During the round to qualify for the finals, Beamon fouled on his first two jumps and needed to stick his last attempt to make the finals. Beamon adjusted his approach and landed at 8.19 meters, which was second best among those entering the finals behind teammate Ralph Boston.

Universitario, but Beamon didn't know the conversion of metric into feet and inches.

Then Beamon's jump posted as 29 feet, 2 ½ inches, sending the American running around in excitement. His jump broke the old record by 55 centimeters, or 21 ¾ inches. The long jump record had only increased by a little more than 8 inches over the previous 35 years. Beamon's world record stood for 23 years before Mike Powell of the USA broke it in 1991 by just 2 ½ inches. Powell's mark remains a world record 29 years later. Beamon's jump at Mexico City in 1968 remains the Olympic record.

TROUBLED YOUTH

Beamon had a troubled childhood. His mother died when he was a baby, and with his stepfather in jail, he was raised by his grandmother in gang territory in Queens, New York. After punching a teacher, he ended up in reform school. At age fifteen, things changed for Beamon when he discovered the long jump and the path that took him to college and Olympic glory.

FANNY BLANKERS-KOEN
NETHERLANDS TRACK AND FIELD

Four Gold Medals at 1948 Olympics

World War II ravaged Europe and caused the cancelation of the Olympic Games in 1940 and again in 1944. So with the Games resuming in London in 1948, the world clamored to see who would be the next international star.

A 30-year-old mother of two from the Netherlands not only stepped up to the challenge, but she also literally ran away with it.

Fanny Blankers-Koen was told she was too old to compete, and some even said she should stay home and take care of her children. Ultimately, she not only competed, but she also dominated the London Games.

Blankers-Koen held world records in six different track and field events before London, but she could choose to enter only up to four Olympic events. Instead of taking the easy road, she chose the four most competitive events.

She started with the 100 meters and won with relative ease. With a gold medal in hand, she wanted to return home to Utrecht. Jan Blankers, who was both her husband and coach, convinced her to stay.

Blankers-Koen won the 80-meter hurdles and then the 200 meters by 0.7 seconds—a mammoth margin for a short race.

LONDON SHOPPING SPREE

Blankers-Koen celebrated her third gold medal in London by going on a shopping spree, and she nearly missed the 4x100-meter relay race. She arrived at Wembley Stadium just 10 minutes before her race, and her teammates had already warmed up. It didn't faze Blankers-Koen, however, as she took the baton and anchored the Dutch to a come-from-behind win.

The Dutch sprinter also ran the anchor leg on the 4x100-meter relay team, taking the baton in fourth place and sprinting her way to cross the finish line first, giving her four gold medals in four events, a record for a woman in track and field at a single Games.

Blankers-Koen returned home to a hero's welcome. Her feats achieved in 1948 make her one of the greatest Olympians in modern history.

MORE THAN A SPRINTER

Blankers-Koen missed a chance at two Olympic Games because of World War II, but she won six European titles—five sprints and one relay—and she set or tied 12 world records, including the long jump and high jump. An excellent athlete as a child, she also competed in swimming, fencing, tennis, ice skating, and gymnastics.

USAIN BOLT
JAMAICA TRACK AND FIELD

Three World Records at 2008 Beijing Games

Usain Bolt will be known as the greatest sprinter of all time for a long while and not just because of what he accomplished at the 2008 Beijing Olympic Games.

In those Games, the Jamaican sprinter blew away his competition in both sprint races and helped the sprint relay team to set another world record. He won three gold medals easily and did it with his captivating smile.

In the 100 meter, Bolt ran the first 15 meters in a lunge position before standing in a tall running position. He pulled way ahead of the pack and even appeared to slow down as he crossed the finish line in 9.69 seconds for a new world record.

Bolt also ran away from the pack in the 200 meter at those same Games, winning by 5 meters in another world record of 19.30 seconds.

The first two runners from the Jamaican 4x100-meter relay team had built a slight lead before Bolt got the baton on the third leg, and the anchor finished it off as Bolt, Nesta Carter, Michael Frater, and Asafa Powell also broke that world record with a time of 37.10 seconds.

"I want to share it with my team," Bolt said after the relay. "It's down to them that I beat the world record today. When you beat the relay world record, you feel four times happier."

Bolt won gold medals in all three sprint races again at the 2012 London Games, and then again at the 2016 Rio de Janeiro Games, becoming the only sprinter in Olympic history to pull off a triple-triple in gold medal performances.

BEFORE AND AFTER HE SPRINTED

Usain Bolt stands 6 feet, 5 inches, and he looked to be a promising high jumper as a teenager. Also before his sprinting talents became evident, Bolt played cricket growing up in Jamaica (he was a fast bowler, of course). Today he heads the Usain Bolt Foundation, which enhances the character of children through education and cultural development.

Jamaican sprinter Usain Bolt broke the world record at the 2008 Beijing Games in each of the 100 meters, 200 meters and 4x100-meter relay races.

NADIA COMĂNECI
ROMANIA GYMNASTICS

Seven Perfect 10 Scores at 1976 Montreal Games

Nadia Comăneci is considered by many to be the best gymnast who ever lived—even transcending recent American Olympian champ Simone Biles and former champion Larisa Latynina from the former Soviet Union.

Comăneci was 14 when she became the first gymnast to achieve a perfect 10 score in the Olympics. At the 1976 Montreal Games, the Romanian competed on the uneven bars, using her energy and power to effortlessly navigate her way through her routine.

Comăneci didn't stop there. She went on to earn a perfect score six more times at those Games, and she won gold medals in the balance beam and individual all-around events. Of her seven perfect scores, four of them came on the uneven bars. Comăneci also won an individual bronze medal for the floor exercise and a silver medal for the team all-around.

However, it was Comăneci's perfect scores that garnered instant international fame. After returning home to her Eastern European nation, she was awarded the Sickle and Hammer Gold Medal and named a Hero of Socialist Labor, which were honors bestowed upon individuals in Warsaw Pact

THE YOUNGEST ALL-AROUND CHAMP

Nadia Comăneci was 14 when she won the individual all-around at the 1976 Olympics, and this is a record that may never be broken. In 1976, gymnasts had to be at least 14 on the first day of competition to be eligible to participate. Gymnasts must now turn at least 16 during the calendar year of the Olympics, meaning 15 is the youngest age any possible champion can be at any current Games.

countries and the Union of Soviet Socialist Republics (USSR) for exceptional achievements and feats. She was named the Associated Press' Female Athlete of the Year in 1976 as well as the BBC Overseas Sports Personality of the Year.

Comăneci won two more Olympic gold medals—in balance beam and floor exercise—at the 1980 Moscow Games and two silver medals in the team and individual all-around events.

WORRY OF DEFECTION

The Romanian government limited Comăneci's travel outside of the country to Los Angeles in 1984 and a few trips to Moscow and Cuba, fearing she might defect. In Los Angeles, she was watched closely to prevent her from defecting to the USA. She did eventually defect in late 1989, escaping from Romania just weeks before the Romanian Revolution.

INGE DE BRUIJN
NETHERLANDS SWIMMING

Three World Records at 2000 Sydney Games

Inge de Bruijn did not surprise anyone by winning three gold medals in three of the top swimming sprints at the 2000 Sydney Games. The way she did it, however, might have amazed them.

The Dutch swimmer made her first Olympic team in 1992 at age 19, but she did not medal at those Barcelona Games. The disappointment of finishing eighth in two races—and not qualifying for the finals in another—led to her placing her swimming career on hold. Then in 1996, she did not even qualify for the national team for The Netherlands.

De Bruijn came roaring back in 2000 leading up to the Olympics, emerging as one of the fastest sprinters in the world. During a two-week stretch in the spring of that year, she beat or tied seven world records. Then came the Sydney Summer Olympic Games, the top stage in the world.

The Dutch swimmer became an international sensation by winning gold in three of the fastest races:

- 50-meter freestyle
- 100-meter freestyle
- 100-meter butterfly

In each of these races, she lowered both the Olympic and world records.

LATE BLOOMER

De Bruijn showed signs of greatness at age 17, winning her first medals at the 1991 European Championships, but it didn't parlay into immediate Olympic success. This fueled her to work even harder. She won her first European Championship title in the 50-meter freestyle at age 26. Then she began setting world records—11 of them before retiring.

She also teamed up with Thamar Henneken, Wilma van Rijn, and Manon van Rooijen to win a silver medal in the 4x100-meter freestyle relay.

Her prowess did not end in Sydney as de Bruijn racked up multiple world championships in the 2001 and 2003 seasons, and she defended her Olympic gold in the 50-meter freestyle at the 2004 Athens Games, where she picked up another silver medal and two bronze medals.

TOP DUTCH SWIMMER

De Bruijn retired in 2007 as one of the top swimmers in her country's history. With four medals in 2000—three of them gold—she became known as "Invincible Inky." She finished her career with 8 Olympic medals, 6 world championship medals and 26 Dutch National Championships.

JANET EVANS
USA SWIMMING

400-Meter Freestyle World Record at 1988 Games

Janet Evans first began swimming laps in the pool when she was two years old, an early start for a kid who would grow up to become one of the best female distance swimmers the world has ever known.

Despite having a small stature and a windmill stroke, Evans broke world records for the 800-meter freestyle and 1,500-meter freestyle when she was only 15 and set the 400-meter freestyle world record just after turning 16.

Evans entered the 1988 Seoul Games as a prohibitive favorite, and she did not disappoint. The teenager broke her own world record in the 400 meters and also won gold in the 800 meters with a new Olympic record, finishing three meters ahead of the second-place swimmer. She also won the gold medal in the 400-meter individual medley, which uses all four strokes—butterfly, backstroke, breaststroke, and freestyle.

Evans returned for the 1992 Barcelona Games, which started with a disappointing silver medal in the 400-meter freestyle. She took out her

WHAT COULD HAVE BEEN

The 1,500-meter freestyle is finally being added to the women's events at the 2020 Tokyo Games. Evans broke the world record in the 1,500 at age 15 in 1987. In 1988 she became the first woman to break the 16-minute mark when she swam it in 15 minutes, 15.521 seconds. Had it been an Olympic event then, Evans could have won two more gold medals.

frustration in the 800-meter freestyle, taking an early lead and never looking back to defend her gold medal, this time winning by 8 meters.

Evans won 22 of 23 races she swam at the 800-meter distance in international events between 1986 and 1995, and she won 25 of 27 races in the 400-meter in that same span.

Her Olympic record in the 400-meter free set at the 1988 Games stood for 28 years, until American Katie Ledecky broke it at the 2016 Rio Games.

EATING WHAT SHE WANTS

Evans swam 12 miles a day and had a teenager's metabolism when she trained for her first Olympic Games in 1988 while still in high school. She claimed that she ate whatever she wanted, no matter how much. As her body matured, however, she adopted a more balanced diet to properly fuel her body for long training sessions.

ALLYSON FELIX
USA TRACK AND FIELD

Only Woman to Win Six Track and Field Gold Medals

Allyson Felix burst on the scene as a teenager at the 2004 Athens Games, finishing second in the 200 meters, her top race. She followed it up with another silver medal in the 200 meters at the 2008 Beijing Games.

Silver is great for some athletes. For Felix, it served as motivation to push herself harder than ever.

"The moments that motivated me the most were losing on the biggest stage, just never forgetting that feeling," Felix said in 2012. "I embrace the defeats because that's what pushed me all those years."

In London, Felix got over the hump and won gold in the 200 meters, beating Jamaican rival Veronica Campbell, who won gold ahead of Felix the previous two Games. This was only the beginning for Felix, who also ran on the 4x100-meter and 4x100-meter relay teams that won gold in London, making Felix the first American woman to win three gold medals in athletics at one Olympics since Florence Griffith-Joyner at the 1988 Seoul Games.

The 4x100-meter relay time of 40.82 seconds smashed a world record set in 1985.

EARLY SUCCESS FOR "CHICKEN LEGS"

Although she was called "chicken legs" by her teammates because of her long, thin legs, Felix has a powerful burst. A little more than two months after her first tryout during her freshman year, Felix finished ninth at the state meet in the 200 meters. She won five state titles in her career and was named the 2003 national girls' high school track athlete of the year.

At the 2016 Rio Games, Felix won two more gold medals in the same relay races and won silver in the 400-meter race.

Felix's six gold and three silver medals represent the most gold by any woman and are just two shy of Carl Lewis' career total of 11, the most by any American in track—male or female.

Felix, showing no signs of slowing down, will have a chance to tie or pass Lewis at the 2020 Tokyo Games.

TURNING PRO EARLY

As a high school phenom, Felix had the option to skip running track in college and sign a professional contract with adidas. As part of the contract she signed with the sportswear company, adidas paid for Felix's tuition to the University of Southern California, where she has since graduated with a degree in elementary education.

DICK FOSBURY
USA TRACK AND FIELD

High Jump Olympic Record at 1968 Games

Failing to qualify for high jump event finals at high school track meets led Dick Fosbury to change his way of thinking, and it ultimately revolutionized jumping.

Fosbury constantly had trouble hitting the minimum mark of 5 feet. The method of jumping taught to him, known as the straddle method, just didn't work for him. He began working on other ways to clear the bar.

The rules of high jump state that the athlete must jump using just one leg, but it doesn't matter how they get over the bar. The Oregonian devised a somewhat unorthodox maneuver where he leaped into the air, face to the sky, and launched his head and neck over the bar first, followed by his legs and feet. He landed on his back, and it became known as the "Fosbury Flop."

The new method also catapulted Fosbury into a new stratosphere of jumpers. He was the state runner-up in his high school senior year and then went on to Oregon State University, while the "flop" became a new wonder in the track and field world.

Fosbury won two college national titles and qualified for the U.S. Olympic team trials in Los Angeles during 1968, where he won first place. The 21-year-old sensation went from high school also-ran to the Olympic Games.

In Mexico City, Fosbury won the gold medal and set a new Olympic record with a jump of 7 feet, 4 ¼ inches, which brought a rousing "Ole!" from the crowd.

JUMPERS ARE STILL FLOPPING

Fosbury's coach at Oregon State was finally convinced he could get better results from the Fosbury Flop, so he filmed his athlete's jumps and studied them. He began teaching that method. Now, the jump Fosbury created out of frustration has become the most-used technique in the world of high jumping.

Dick Fosbury revolutionized the high jump when he devised his own method of clearing the bar. His unorthodox approach became known as the "Fosbury Flop."

FLORENCE GRIFFITH-JOYNER
USA TRACK AND FIELD

World Record in 200 Meters at 1988 Seoul Games

Florence Griffith, who qualified for the 1980 Olympic team but couldn't compete in Moscow because of the U.S. boycott, competed in her first Olympics in 1984 in her hometown of Los Angeles. She won the silver medal in the 200 meters. Despite a nice finish, it was her flashy, long fingernails that became the topic of her appearance at the Games.

She married 1984 triple-jump gold medalist Al Joyner after those Olympics, and Griffith added Joyner to the end of her name. She became known simply as "Flo-Jo."

Flo-Jo kept improving over the next Olympic cycle, and she would become part of Olympic lore in 1988. At the U.S. Olympic trials, she ran the 100 meters in 10.49 seconds, obliterating the former world record by three-tenths of a second. Her time was faster than the men's national records in Ireland, New Zealand, Norway, and Turkey at the time.

At the 1988 Seoul Games, Flo-Jo set an Olympic record in the 100 meters and a world record in the 200 meters while winning gold medals in both events. Amazingly enough, her records in these races have stood for 31 years heading into the 2020 Olympics.

Flo-Jo won a third gold medal in Seoul for the 4x100-meter relay. Her three gold medals at one Olympics were not matched until Allyson Felix pulled the trifecta in the same events at the 2012 London Games.

Ten years after her feats in Seoul, Flo-Jo died suddenly in her sleep from an epileptic seizure at the age of 38.

Florence Griffith-Joyner, with her dazzling fingernails and smooth sprinting stride, set the current Olympic records in the 100 meters and 200 meters at the 1988 Seoul Games.

BEFORE SHE WAS FLO-JO

Florence Griffith ran one year of track at California State University at Northridge before she dropped out to take a job at a bank to help support her family. Bob Kersee, who coached Griffith at Northridge, took a track coach job at UCLA and found financial aid for her to return to college. Griffith graduated from UCLA in 1983 with a degree in psychology.

YELENA ISINBAYEVA
RUSSIA TRACK AND FIELD

Pole Vault World Record at 2008 Beijing Games

Yelena Isinbayeva had already clinched a gold medal and successfully defended her Olympic pole vault title earned in 2004, but she wanted more on one August night in Beijing. With 91,000 spectators looking down upon the track and field events, Isinbayeva asked the bar to be raised to 5.05 meters.

All other events in the stadium known as the "Bird's Nest" had already concluded, so the crowd watched only the Russian athlete. Isinbayeva cleared the height that's equal to 16 feet, 6 ¾ inches, to set the new world record, breaking the one she set the previous month in Monaco.

Isinbayeva entered the pole vault world at just the right time. She grew up in Russia aspiring to be a gymnast, but she grew too tall, so she shifted her focus to becoming the best pole vault athlete possible.

Pole vault became an event for women at the Olympics at the 2000 Sydney Games, right as Isinbayeva's interest in the sport was piqued. She first broke the world record in 2003 at an event in Gateshead, England, besting American Stacy Dragila's previous mark by half an inch.

BREAKING HER OWN RECORDS

Isinbayeva broke her first world record in 2003, and she has broken the record 16 more times since then. She's known as the "Pole Vault Queen," the undisputed champion of women's pole vault. She broke the world record six times in England, twice in Switzerland, and once in several other countries. She never broke the world record in her home country.

Isinbayeva went on to break the world record 17 times, which is a record in itself. Her last, and the current, record was a vault of 5.06 meters in 2009. After winning bronze at the 2012 London Games, Isinbayeva retired in 2016, despite having the highest vault in the world that year.

She is the only female to ever win two Olympic gold medals in the pole vault.

UNABLE TO COMPETE IN 2016

The International Association of Athletics Federation (IAAF) banned Russia's track and field athletes from competing in the 2016 Rio Games for multiple doping scandals, but Isinbayeva appealed, saying she was one of the "clean" athletes. Her appeals were denied.

MICHAEL JOHNSON
USA TRACK AND FIELD

Set Two Records at 1996 Olympic Games

Michael Johnson never intended to become a track star; it just happened. Growing up as the youngest of five children in Dallas, Texas, he focused on academics ahead of athletics.

He attended Baylor University, and that's where coach Clyde Hart discovered Johnson, who had untapped potential at the time. Johnson had an upright running style with a short stride, which brought on his nickname, "The Duck." He set the school record in the 200 meters at Baylor, and it was only the beginning of a marvelous career.

Johnson became the world champion in the 200 meters during 1991, but he missed the race at the 1992 Barcelona Games after food poisoning sidetracked him. He recuperated and won gold on the 4x100-meter relay team.

Johnson was at full strength for the 1996 Atlanta Games, and he had a home country cheering for him. Wearing specially-made gold colored track shoes, Johnson pulled off an unprecedented feat of winning both the 200 meters and 400 meters at the Games. The 200–400 double had never happened before Johnson did it, nor has it since. His 200-meter time remained a world record until Usain Bolt broke it 12 years later, and his 400-meter time was also an Olympic record.

Johnson ran again at the 2000 Sydney Games, where he defended his Olympic title in the 400 meters. He finished his career with four gold medals on the track, but he will always be remembered for those gold-colored shoes as he ran before the home crowd.

ONLY GOLD FOR JOHNSON

The image of Johnson running in gold colored shoes may be the first thing some people remember about him, but his running was pure gold. Between his Olympic and world championship appearances, Johnson amassed eight world titles and four Olympic medals, and he always stood at the top of the podium, as never once did the Texan settle for silver or bronze.

Michael Johnson wore specially made golden track shoes at the 1996 Atlanta Games, and he was pure gold. He set a world record in the 200 meters.

JACKIE JOYNER-KERSEE USA TRACK AND FIELD

World Record Heptathlon at 1988 Seoul Games

Jackie Joyner-Kersee was so dominant in the heptathlon at the 1988 Seoul Games that her record score still hasn't been beaten. Joyner-Kersee in 1987 became the first woman to ever break 7,000 points in the event. Then at Seoul, she set the benchmark that has stood for more than 30 years.

Joyner-Kersee won three of the seven events outright and tied for first in another. Here's a breakdown of her performance in Seoul:

- 100 meters (1st)
- 200 meters (1st)
- Long jump (1st)
- High jump (1st, tied)
- Shot put (2nd)
- Javelin throw (4th)
- 800 meters (5th)

This record performance more than made up for her 1984 Olympics result, entering as the heptathlon favorite but coming up short and winning the silver medal. She also won the gold medal in the long jump at the 1988 Games.

Her leap of 7.40 meters at the 1988 Games remains an Olympic record, and her jump of 7.49 meters in 1994 is still the second-best jump ever among female athletes.

Joyner-Kersee went on to defend her heptathlon gold medal at the 1992 Barcelona Games.

Her athletic achievements earned her the title "The Greatest Female Athlete of the 20th Century" from *Sports Illustrated*.

Not to get lost in the shuffle are Joyner-Kersee's basketball skills. She was a four-year starter at UCLA and was among the career leaders in scoring, rebounds, and games played.

"I strive to be a Jackie of all trades," Joyner-Kersee said. "I am an individual who has accomplished a great deal through athletics."

GIVING BACK TO HER COMMUNITY

A native of St. Louis, Missouri, Jackie Joyner-Kersee used her status of one of the greatest female athletes of the 20th century to start the Jackie Joyner-Kersee Foundation, which aims to assist at-risk children to better themselves through education, athletics, and leadership in low-income communities throughout East St. Louis and around the country.

Jackie Joyner-Kersee finished in the top five in all seven events of the heptathlon at the 1988 Seoul Games. Her 7,291 points remain a world record.

SAWAO KATO
JAPAN GYMNASTICS

Eight Career Gold Medals Over Three Olympics

Long before Sawao Kato launched, twisted, tumbled, and turned into Japanese Olympic lore, he was just a child who excelled at school. He was a reluctant athlete, but that changed the day he walked into a gymnastics gym.

He applied the traits that made him a fantastic academic—hard work and the ability to learn quickly—and he soared onto the national scene.

Kato strived for perfection in everything thing he did, and he made the national team by the time he was 18 and studying at Kyoiku University in Tokyo.

Kato made his Olympic debut at the 1968 Mexico City Games, where he won three gold medals and one bronze—all while battling an injury to his Achilles tendon that almost ended his career.

Kato won the individual all-around and the floor exercise events, and he helped his team win the team competition. Kato won three more gold medals at the 1972 Munich Games, including the individual all-around, parallel bars, and another team title. At the 1976 Montreal Games, he guided his country to a third consecutive team

THE PROFESSOR

Kato halted his competitive career after the 1976 Montreal Games, having established himself as one of the greatest Olympians of all time. He went back to school and became a professor at his university alma mater, which had since been renamed Tsukuba University. He was eventually named professor emeritus, meaning he was well respected, and earned tenure.

title while raking in another individual gold medal in parallel bars.

Before he accomplished his Olympic feats over an eight-year period, the Soviets were the top gymnasts in the world, but Kato brought Japan into the international limelight. His 8 Olympic gold medals and 12 overall medals are both the most by any male gymnast in history, earning him the designation of "Japan's Greatest Olympian."

STAYING INVOLVED

Although he stepped away from competing in the sport to focus on his teaching career, Japan's greatest Olympian remained involved in gymnastics. He was the vice president of the Technical Commission for the International Gymnastics Federation until 1998, and he's a member of the Gymnastics Hall of Fame.

LARISA LATYNINA
USSR GYMNASTICS

18 Career Medals Over Three Olympics

Long before American swimmer Michael Phelps set the new benchmark for Olympic medals in a career, Soviet gymnast Larisa Latynina became the most-decorated athlete in the history of the modern Olympics.

Latynina was from southern Ukraine, which at the time was part of the USSR. (Ukraine has once again become an independent country.)

She won a career 18 Olympic medals, including 9 gold medals. She did it over three Olympic Games on three different continents—also something of a rarity in its time.

Latynina stormed onto the Olympic scene at the 1956 Melbourne Games in Australia, winning four gold medals, a bronze, and a silver. She took individual titles in the all-around, vault, and floor exercise events, and she won a gold in the team competition.

She defended her gold medals for team competition and floor exercise in both the 1960 Games in Rome, Italy and the 1964 Tokyo Games. She also won a second gold for the all-around in 1960.

Latynina won seven other medals in Rome and Tokyo in the uneven bars, balance beam, vault, and team portable

TOUGH CHILDHOOD

Latynina's father left the family when she was just 11 months old. He was killed during the Battle of Stalingrad, one of the bloodiest battles of World War II, in which Russian forces fought the Nazis. Latynina's mother was not educated and worked as a cleaner for a day job and also as a security guard for a second job to provide for Latynina.

apparatus. She medaled in every event at all three games with the sole exception of balance beam at Melbourne.

Her 18 medals were the record for any Olympian in history until Phelps (who won 28) broke it at the 2012 London Games, but they are still an all-time best for any gymnast in modern Olympic history. Her 9 gold medals is a record as well.

SUCCESSFUL SOVIET COACH AND OLYMPIC COORDINATOR

Latynina became a coach for the Soviet team after she retired, and the success of USSR gymnastics continued. They won the all-around team title at the1968, 1972, and 1976 Olympic Games. When Moscow hosted the 1980 Summer Olympics, Latynina was the organizer for the gymnastics competitions.

KATIE LEDECKY
USA SWIMMING

Two World Records at 2016 Rio Games

Katie Ledecky was barely 15 when she made her presence known on the international stage, winning the gold medal in the 800-meter freestyle at the 2012 London Games.

To prove she was no fluke, Ledecky followed it up by becoming the most-decorated female Olympian of the 2016 Rio Games. In Rio, she won four gold medals and one silver medal, but it was her performance in the 400-meter and 800-meter freestyle races that shined brightest.

Ledecky shattered the world record by swimming the 400-meter freestyle in 3 minutes, 56.46 seconds, which was 5 seconds ahead of the second-place finisher. "3:56 was the goal I set after Barcelona 2013 (World Championships), so it feels really good," she said after the race.

In the 800-meter freestyle, Ledecky swam 8:04.79 to beat the old world record by 2 seconds, and she was 11 seconds ahead of the silver medalist.

She also won the 200-meter freestyle, making her the first to win all three of those races in one Olympic Games since 1968. In that race, she needed every bit of moxie to edge Sweden's Sarah Sjöström.

"I'm pretty sure that's the closest I've come to throwing up in the middle of a race," she said.

Ledecky also swam the anchor leg of the 4x200-meter freestyle relay and was a member of the 4x100-meter relay that finished second for silver, just behind Australia.

Ledecky was only 19 in Rio, and as the world record holder in three events, she is a huge favorite to add to her haul in Tokyo in 2020.

SCHOOLING THE COMPETITION

After her record-setting performances at the 2016 Rio Games, Katie Ledecky enrolled at Stanford University and twice helped lead the Cardinals to an NCAA women's national championship. Ledecky won five individual championships and three more on freestyle relay teams. After her sophomore year, she gave up her amateur status to turn pro.

Katie Ledecky wins the 200-meter freestyle race at the 2016 Rio Games to cap a trifecta of gold medal performances in the 200-, 400-, and 800-meter freestyle.

CARL LEWIS
USA TRACK AND FIELD

Nine Career Gold Medals, Four at 1984 Games

Carl Lewis began breaking national track and field records when he was still in high school. He became an NCAA champion, but he catapulted to real fame during the 1984 Los Angeles Summer Olympics.

Lewis accomplished something only Jesse Owens achieved before him and that was to win four gold medals in track and field events at one Olympics:

- 100 meters
- 200 meters
- 4x100-meter relay
- Long jump

Lewis' first leap of 8.54 meters (28 feet, 0 inches) was good enough to win the long jump gold medal, and he knew it. Lewis fouled on jump two and skipped his next four jumps, which drew "boos" from the home crowd that wanted to see him challenge Bob Beamon's record of 8.90 meters (29 feet, 2 ½ inches).

Having already won gold in the 100 meters, Lewis claimed he was saving his legs for the 200 meters and the relay. He went on to victory in the 200 with an Olympic record of 19.80 seconds, and the relay squad set a world record with a time of 37.83 seconds.

Lewis went on to compete in three more Olympics, winning the long jump event in each of them. He finished second in the 100 meters to Canada's Ben Johnson at the 1988 Seoul Games. Johnson, however, later tested positive for steroids, and his gold medal was stripped and awarded to Lewis, whose time (9.92 seconds) became the new Olympic record.

At the 1992 Barcelona Games, Lewis anchored the 4x100-meter relay team that ran a world record time of 37.40 seconds—a record that stood for 16 years.

POTENTIAL FOR MORE GLORY

Carl Lewis broke the national high school long jump record in 1979, just days after his graduation. He went on to compete at the University of Houston, where he won the national championship in the long jump in 1980. He was slated to participate in the 1980 Moscow Games in the long jump and 4x100-meter relay, but the American boycott prevented him from competing.

American sprinter Carl Lewis won four gold medals at the 1984 Los Angeles Games, tying a mark set by Jesse Owens. He accomplished it in the same events as well— 100 meters, 200 meters, 4x100-meter relay, and long jump.

GREG LOUGANIS
USA DIVING

Back-to-Back Double Golds at 1984 & 1988 Games

Greg Louganis is considered to be the greatest Olympic diving champion of all time. At the 1984 Los Angeles Games he pulled off a remarkable double-gold feat, winning both the 3-meter springboard and the 10-meter platform events.

Although he defended both medals at the 1988 Seoul Games, it was a mishap at the pool in South Korea that will always be remembered.

On the 3-meter springboard for the preliminary round, Louganis' dive was a reverse two-and-a-half somersault in pike position. The back of his head clipped the board before he entered the pool. He sustained a large gash in his scalp, and blood seeped into the pool.

Amazingly, Louganis was back in the pool 35 minutes later to finish his preliminary dives. "We worked too long and hard to get there, and I don't want to give up without a fight," he said.

Louganis made the finals and once again won gold, even nailing that same "Dive of Death," as he called it.

Louganis was a classical dance student growing up. This is the likely foundation for his artistic and elegant dives. He first won a silver medal in the platform at the 1976 Montreal Games when he was just 16. He did not get the chance to dive in 1980 because of the U.S. boycott of the Moscow Games. In 1984, he became the first Olympian in 54 years to win double gold in the springboard and platform. He also won six world championships aside from the Olympics.

He has most recently become an activist for lesbian, gay, bisexual, and transgender (LGBT) rights and human immunodeficiency virus (HIV) awareness.

WHAT COULD HAVE BEEN IN 1980

Greg Louganis is one of hundreds of American athletes who missed the 1980 Moscow Games because of the U.S. boycott. As he was the world's top diver at the time, Louganis would have had the chance to win his first double gold had he competed in Moscow. It is possible that he could have won an unprecedented three double-golds in the event.

Greg Louganis clips his head during a dive off the 3-meter springboard at the 1988 Seoul Games. He comes back to win the gold medal.

MISTY MAY-TREANOR & KERRI WALSH JENNINGS USA BEACH VOLLEYBALL

Three Gold Medals, 21 Consecutive Wins at Games

Beach volleyball is a sport that gained popularity in the 1960s for its cool, laid-back style of playing an indoor sport on some sand next to the ocean. The sport became international, and then it became commercialized.

Beach volleyball first debuted at the 1996 Atlanta Games, but no one has dominated it like Kerri Walsh Jennings and Misty May-Treanor. The duo teamed up at the 2004 Athens Games and swept their way to a gold medal, winning seven consecutive matches. They did the same thing at the 2008 Beijing Games and again at the 2012 London Games.

Both players competed in the 2000 Sydney Games, but not on the same team, nor the same arena. May-Treanor played beach volleyball with partner Holly McPeak and Walsh Jennings played on the women's indoor team. Neither won a medal.

Misty May and Kerri Walsh joined together on the beach tour in 2001, and they became an unstoppable force. They entered the 2004 Games

with a 90-game winning streak, and they rolled through the competition for gold.

They entered Beijing having won 18 consecutive tournaments and 101 straight matches. Once again, they easily won gold.

The Americans won their third gold in London. May-Treanor retired after the 2012 Olympics and Walsh Jennings won a bronze at the 2016 Rio de Janeiro Games with new teammate April Ross. Though the sport has only been around for six Olympics, Kerri Walsh Jennings and Misty May-Treanor will go down as one of the greatest duos of all time.

COLLEGE BEACH VOLLEYBALL

The success of players like May-Treanor and Walsh Jennings led to a spike in beach volleyball's popularity, causing the NCAA to make it an emerging sport and in 2015, an official championship sport. Olympic and pro beach volleyball paved the way for more than 40 colleges to sanction varsity programs, the threshold for consideration as a championship sport.

Americans Misty May-Treanor and Kerri Walsh Jennings face China in the gold medal match of the 2008 Beijing Games. Here are the waning moments of their victory.

IAN MILLAR
CANADA EQUESTRIAN

10 Olympic Appearances Over a 40-year Span

Ian Millar doesn't have a chest full of medals for his lifetime of competing in Olympic equestrian jumping, but he has an Olympic record that's quite impressive.

Millar competed in 10 Summer Olympics, starting with the 1972 Munich Games and ending with the 2012 London Games. The only one he missed was the 1980 Moscow Games during Canada's boycott that summer.

Known as "Captain Canada," Millar broke the record in 2012, when he rode the horse named Star Power in London. His 10th appearance surpassed the previous record of nine Olympics by Austrian sailor Hubert Raudaschl, who competed from 1964 to 1996.

Although Millar has only one Olympic medal, a team silver from the 2008 Beijing Games, his 10 Olympics appearances remain a record.

During the 2008 Beijing Games, Millar was 61 when he rode In Style in a flawless round to put Team Canada in first place. The Americans eventually won the gold medal, but the Canadians held onto the silver medal for Millar's only podium finish in the Olympics.

Millar finished just off of the Olympic medal podium two other times with fourth-place finishes in team competition. His best individual performance was his last, when he finished ninth in London.

Millar continued riding internationally after that at the World Equestrian Games in 2014, and then the Pan American Games of 2015, where he won a team gold medal and placed 16th in the individual event.

Millar retired from international competition on May 1, 2019.

IAN AND BIG BEN

Ian Millar purchased Big Ben for $45,000 in 1979, and the horse began a career of show jumping with Millar in 1984. Millar won more than 40 Grand Prix titles on Big Ben and rode the large horse in three consecutive Olympics (1984, 1988, and 1992). Millar rode Big Ben to Pan American Games titles in both the team and individual events in 1987.

PAN AMERICAN SUCCESS

Millar was an accomplished equestrian jumper outside of the Olympics. He won at least one medal in the Pan American Games in five different decades. His first was in 1979, when he won an individual bronze and team silver while riding Brother Sam, and his last was in 2015, when he won individual gold riding Dixson.

PAAVO NURMI
FINLAND TRACK AND FIELD

Set Two World Records Less Than Two Hours Apart

Paavo Nurmi accomplished two remarkable feats in Summer Olympics history. First, he won nine career gold medals and three silver medals. Then there was his performance in Paris at the 1924 Games, when he won five of those gold medals.

The distance runner, who was part of the talented group known as the "Flying Finns," didn't just run one particular distance. Nurmi ran everything from the 3,000-meter team event to the 10,000 meters, cross-country, and the steeplechase.

Nurmi made his Olympic debut at the 1920 Antwerp Games, where he won three gold medals and one silver medal. He won the 10,000-meter race, the individual cross-country, and also the gold in team cross-country.

As well as his first Olympics went, it was at the 1924 Paris Games when Nurmi showed the world his dominance and versatility. In five races over just six days, he won five gold medals in:

- 5,000 meters
- Cross-country team
- 3,000-meters team
- Cross-country individual
- 1,500 meters

SIMULTANEOUS WORLD RECORDS

Nurmi is the only runner in history to hold the records in the 1,500, 5,000, and 10,000 meters—all at the same time. The Flying Finn set a total of 22 world records in every distance from the 1,500 meters to the 20,000 meters in his career. Additionally, he never lost a cross-country race.

He not only ran the 1,500-meter and 5,000-meter races on the same day, but Nurmi ran the 5,000 less than two hours after the 1,500 and set world records in both.

In the 1928 Amsterdam Games, Nurmi won gold in the 10,000 meters and picked up silver medals in the 5,000-meter race and 3,000-meter steeplechase. The 1928 Olympics turned out to be his last after the IAAF deemed him a professional runner, thus halting his amateur status to qualify for any more Games.

PROFESSIONAL STATUS

After Nurmi's international success through the 1928 Games, he was invited all over the world to become the main attraction at athletic events. Prior to the 1932 Los Angeles Games, the IAAF said his participation as an "attraction" caused them to brand him as a professional, preventing the Flying Finn from defending his gold medal in the 10,000 meters.

JESSE OWENS
USA TRACK AND FIELD

Four Gold Medals at 1936 Paris Games

Jesse Owens became known as the greatest and most famous track and field athlete of his lifetime. His heroics at the 1936 Berlin Games are etched in Olympic lore. He won four gold medals in:

- 200 meters
- 4x100-meter relay
- Long jump
- 100 meters

Along the way, Owens set three world records and broke or tied nine Olympic records. He did it in Nazi Germany in front of Adolf Hitler, who wanted to use these Games as a showcase for Aryan racial supremacy. In the end, Owens blistered the competition and was dubbed a hero by the Germans.

Owens battled oppression and racism long before. Born the youngest of 10 children to a sharecropper in Alabama, Jesse was 9 when his family moved to Ohio during the Great Migration of African Americans moving north from the segregated southern states.

Owens worked a variety of jobs, but he loved running. He first gained notoriety when he tied a world record in the

NO HERO'S WELCOME

Owens considered boycotting the 1936 Berlin Games in Nazi Germany. As it turned out, the crowds in Germany cheered Owens for his record setting performances. It was when he returned home that he faced discrimination. Despite his four gold medals, only white athletes were invited to the White House to meet President Franklin Roosevelt.

100-yard dash in 9.4 seconds at the 1933 National High School Championship.

He attended Ohio State University and ran for the Buckeyes, becoming known as the "Buckeye Bullet." Owens won four NCAA titles in 1935 and again in1936. Being a great athlete, however, did not insulate Owens from the realities of the time. He had to live off campus with other black athletes, had to order out food or eat at blacks-only restaurants, and had to stay at blacks-only hotels.

Growing up dealing with such prejudices ultimately set him up to defy Hitler on a worldwide stage.

GREATEST 45 MINUTES IN SPORTS

While competing for Ohio State University at the Big Ten Championship meet on May 25, 1935, at Ferry Field in Ann Arbor, Michigan, Jesse Owens pulled off one of the most amazing feats in sports history. In a span of just 45 minutes, Owens set five world records and tied a sixth. His record long jump that day of 8.13 meters stood for 25 years.

MICHAEL PHELPS
USA SWIMMING

28 Olympic Medals, 23 Gold, 8 Gold at 2008 Games

Michael Phelps first splashed onto the international scene at the 2000 Summer Olympics in Sydney, when at age 15 he became the youngest American male Olympian in 68 years.

Phelps didn't medal in Sydney, but he made the team every four-year Olympic cycle through 2016, making him the first American male swimmer to qualify for five Olympic Games. Through the next four Games, he reached the medal podium 28 times, amassing 23 gold medals in the process.

Although no athlete, in any country or in any sport, may ever reach his career-record medal count, equally impressive was his 2008 performance in Beijing, where he won eight gold medals—which is still an Olympic record.

At those 2008 Games, Phelps won gold in five individual events and three more on relay teams. In the process, he set seven world records, eight American records, and eight Olympic records.

He won every race he swam in 2008:

- 100-meter butterfly
- 200-meter butterfly

Fifteen-year-old Michael Phelps broke his first world record at the 2001 world championship trials in Austin, Texas, when he swam the semifinals of the 200-meter butterfly. He then broke his own world record to win the world championship that summer in the 200-meter butterfly at age 16.

- 200-meter freestyle
- 200-meter individual medley
- 400-meter individual medley
- 4x100-meter freestyle relay
- 4x100-meter freestyle relay
- 4x100-meter medley relay

Phelps also won six gold medals and two bronze medals at the 2004 Athens Games; four gold medals and two silvers at the 2012 London Games; and five gold medals and another silver medal at the 2016 Rio Games.

Michael Phelps will go down as not only one of the best swimmers in history but also perhaps the most decorated Olympian who will ever compete.

PHYSIQUE AND EFFORT

Phelps had a strong work ethic, which drove him to be one of the best swimmers to ever dive into a pool. However, the natural dimensions of his body also attributed to his prowess. Phelps is 6 feet, 4 inches, and his wingspan spreads 6 feet, 7 inches, from fingertip to fingertip. His shoe size is 14, and his large feet create a fin-like effect in the water.

WILMA RUDOLPH
USA TRACK AND FIELD

Three World Records at 1960 Rome Games

Wilma Rudolph ran track in high school to stay busy when it wasn't basketball season, but it was from the basketball court that she was recruited to run track.

The track coach from nearby Tennessee State University first discovered Rudolph, and he invited her to join his team's summer training program—just two years after shedding a leg brace she wore after contracting infantile paralysis because of polio.

After Rudolph attended her first running camp, she competed in an Amateur Athletic Union (AAU) meet in Philadelphia, where she won all nine events she entered. She became so good so fast that she began competing with the college track team at AAU events while she was still in high school.

Two years after her first running camp and while still only a junior in high school, Rudolph competed at the 1956 Olympic team trials, making the U.S. team.

At the 1956 Melbourne Games, Rudolph won a bronze medal as part of the women's 4x100-meter relay team. That success, coupled with her youth, set the stage for what was to come the following Olympics.

THE "BLACK GAZELLE"

After her dominating world record performance in the sprints during the 1960 Rome Games, Rudolph became known as the "fastest woman in the world." The European Press took it a step further, calling her the "black gazelle" because of her speed and grace on the track.

Rudolph once again made the U.S. Olympic team for the 1960 Rome Games, and she shined on the brightest stage of all. She won gold medals with world records in the following:

- 4x100-meter relay
- 200 meters
- 100 meters

With the Olympics gaining popularity due to TV coverage, the little girl who had trouble walking as a child became an international sensation.

CHILDHOOD ILLNESS AND DISEASE

Wilma Rudolph was quite sick as a child. She was born prematurely and weighed just 4 ½ pounds, and she had scarlet fever and pneumonia as a child. She later contracted the polio virus, which left her partially paralyzed. Although getting medical treatment was difficult for African Americans during the 1940s, she ultimately overcame her obstacles.

MARK SPITZ
USA SWIMMING

Seven World Records at 1972 Munich Games

Mark Spitz was a worldwide swimming sensation in the youth ranks long before he became a teenager. At age 10, he held 17 national age-group records and a world record.

At age 22, Spitz entered the 1968 Mexico City Games as a favorite to win seven individual gold medals as he had already set 10 world records. The Mexico City Games, however, were somewhat disappointing as he won just two relay gold medals and two individual silver medals.

Spitz enrolled at collegiate swimming powerhouse Indiana University and trained four years under famed coach James "Doc" Counsilman. Spitz racked up eight NCAA individual championships, setting himself up for the 1972 Munich Games as a favorite to strike heavy gold.

Spitz, a native Californian and butterfly specialist, began Munich by winning the 200-meter butterfly in a world-record time of 2:00.07. He went on to win six more gold medals, all with world-record times.

He set records in the following events::

- 200-meter butterfly
- 200-meter freestyle
- 100-meter butterfly
- 100-meter freestyle

PALESTINIAN TERROR ATTACK IN MUNICH

Spitz is Jewish, so he was understandably nervous during the Munich Games when on the morning of September 5, 1972, Palestinian terrorists broke into the athletes' lodging area, killed two Israeli athletes, and took nine others hostage. Spitz did a press conference that morning and then left for London, skipping the closing ceremonies.

- 4x100-meter freestyle relay
- 4x200-meter freestyle relay
- 4x100-meter medley relay

With this feat, Spitz became the first athlete to win seven gold medals in one modern Olympic Games, and he accomplished it during an era when swimmers didn't wear caps, goggles, or full-body suits.

Spitz retired from swimming after the 1972 Munich Games with 11 total medals, 9 of which were gold.

ATTEMPTED HOLLYWOOD CAREER

After the 1972 Games, Spitz became a product pitchman, and his agent tried to parlay the athlete's good looks into an acting career. However, after a few stints of less-than-stellar performances on television shows, the Hollywood scene dried up, as did most of the products endorsements. Spitz did go on to work as a broadcaster for several years.

TEÓFILO STEVENSON
CUBA BOXING

Three Gold Medals in Three Olympics

Teófilo Stevenson followed his father's footsteps and began training at an open-air Cuban boxing gym when he was young. He had incredible fighting instincts and soon began winning junior titles.

Great boxers typically emerged from Cuba, and Stevenson may have been the best of them all. He became the first boxer in the history of the modern Olympics to win three gold medals in three consecutive Olympics, and all in the same weight class—the heavyweight class—which later became the super-heavyweight division.

His Olympic debut came at the 1972 Munich Games, and he knocked down Poland's Ludwik Denderys in the first 30 seconds. The fight was stopped because of a large cut next to Ludwik's eye. Stevenson knocked out his next two opponents to make the finals, and he was awarded the gold medal when his opponent didn't show up because of an injury.

In the 1976 Montreal Games, Stevenson defeated his first three opponents in an astounding total time of 7 minutes, 22 seconds. In the gold medal fight against Romanian Mircea Simon,

THE RUSSIAN RIVAL

Stevenson had a short, but quite memorable, rivalry with Igor Vysotsky of the Soviet Union. The two only met twice—once in Cuba during 1973 and again in Minsk in 1976. Of Stevenson's career 332–22–8 record, the Soviet was the only one to beat him twice, including a knockout.

the fighters made it to the third round before Simon's managers threw in the towel.

In the 1980 Moscow Games, Stevenson defeated the Soviet Union's Pyotr Zayev for his third gold medal.

Stevenson maintained his amateur status through the late 1980s, but Cuba boycotted both the 1984 Los Angeles Games and 1988 Seoul Games, perhaps denying Stevenson a chance at two more gold medals. Stevenson also won three world championships.

REFUSAL TO TURN PRO

After the 1976 Montreal Games and with two gold medals in his grasp, Stevenson was a hero in Cuba. He was even called the country's "most famous figure after Fidel Castro," by the British Broadcasting Company. Stevenson ignored lucrative offers from the USA to turn professional but did get several cars and two houses from the Cuban government.

TEAM CHINA
CHINA TABLE TENNIS

53 Total Medals, 28 Gold Medals Since 1988

Table tennis became an Olympic sport at the 1988 Seoul Games, and the Chinese national team has dominated the event. Although its women's team has been slightly more successful since the sport made its debut, the Chinese teams are the gold standard for both sexes.

China has won 53 medals overall since 1988, and more than half of those are gold. They have won 28 gold medals out of a possible 32 since the Seoul Games. When China hosted the 2008 Beijing Games, the team did something even more remarkable. For the only time in Olympic history, one country swept both team titles and all three individual medals for both men and women at one Olympics—China.

China has also won 17 silver medals in table tennis, with 15 of those second-place finishes coming behind a fellow countryman who won gold.

The Chinese dominance has not been just a handful of players either. Only three players—all women—have won four gold medals:

- Deng Yaping (1992–1996)
- Wang Nan (2000–2008), also won a silver medal
- Zhang Yining (2004–2008)

NATIONAL SPORT

Chinese leader Mao Tse-Tung declared table tennis as the national sport of China during the 1950s. He did so because it is a cheap sport to play, does not require a lot of space to play, and it was not a popular sport in Western countries. Now almost every school has a team, and tables can be found in parks. More than 300 million people play the sport.

A total of 24 players from China have won either a team or an individual gold medal.

More than 300 million people play table tennis in China, and about 20 million of them play competitively, so making the Olympic team is not easy.

The Chinese national team undergoes intense training that can last 7 hours a day, and coaches constantly analyze competition from all over the world so that they can have a strategy going into each match.

MIXED DOUBLES IN TOKYO

The doubles competition for both men and women was eliminated after the 2004 Athens Games, and it has just been a team event for the last three Olympics. A mixed doubles team will make its debut at the 2020 Tokyo Games, and China will likely be the favorite to win gold.

JENNY THOMPSON
USA SWIMMING

Most Women's Swimming Medals in Olympic History

American swimmer Jenny Thompson accomplished an unmatched Olympic feat for a woman by winning eight gold medals, all in relay events. Although her gold medal count is lofty, it could have been even higher if it were not for a couple of disappointments.

Thompson was a sprint specialist in both the freestyle and butterfly. She set individual world records in other international competitions, winning three world championship gold medals along the way. At the Olympics, however, individual success was always just out of reach.

At her Olympic debut at the 1992 Barcelona Games, she hoped to win a medal in all five events she entered. After finishing fifth in the 50-meter freestyle and not qualifying for the 200-meter freestyle finals, she settled for three medals:

- 4x100-meter freestyle relay (gold)
- 4x100 medley relay (gold)
- 100-meter freestyle (silver)

The 100-meter freestyle result was particularly disappointing as Thompson held the world record in the event at the time.

At the 1996 Atlanta Games, she won three gold medals—two in the freestyle sprint relays and another in the medley relay. She duplicated those gold medals at the 2000 Sydney Games but settled for a bronze medal in the 100-meter freestyle. Stunningly, she finished fifth in the 100-meter butterfly, having come into Sydney as the world record holder.

At the 2004 Athens Games, Thompson won a pair of relay silver medals.

Her 12 Olympic swimming medals are still the most by any female in history.

DR. THOMPSON

After graduating from Stanford University, Thompson earned her medical degree from Columbia University College of Physicians and Surgeons. After an internship in New York, Dr. Jenny Thompson went on to become an anesthesiologist and surgeon, and now she practices medicine at Maine Medical Center in Portland, Maine.

Check out this video that highlights two-time U.S. Swimmer of the Year Jenny Thompson's career.

LIU XIANG
CHINA TRACK AND FIELD

World Record in 110-Meter Hurdles at 2004 Games

Liu Xiang of China stunned the world when he won the 100-meter hurdles at the 2004 Athens Games. It wasn't just because he became the first Chinese man to win a gold medal in track in the modern Olympics or that he was not expected to win a medal at all. It was also because Liu equaled a world record in the process.

Liu began training on the hurdles just 6 years before the Athens Games. He started his career in the high jump, but bone tests showed he would not grow as tall as the more prolific jumpers, causing him to decide to switch events.

His given name, Xiang, means "to soar." At Athens, he soared down the track and cleared each hurdle to set the Olympic record and tie the world record with a time of 12.91 seconds.

Liu broke his own world record in 2006 when he became the first person to break the 12.9-second mark. He won gold at the 2007 world championships and looked poised to defend his gold medal before an adoring home crowd at the 2008 Beijing Games.

During his first heat in Beijing, another runner had a false start, and Liu walked off the track after that. He later revealed he had an injury

HOME DISAPPOINTMENT AND CONFUSION

After Liu walked off the track during his first heat in the 110-meter hurdles at the 2008 Beijing Games, he did not appear publicly to explain what had happened to a crestfallen nation. He instead sent his manager, Sun Haiping, to give a tearful press conference explaining the injury. Liu did apologize to his fans in a recorded interview the following day.

in his right Achilles tendon, which would have prevented from running at 100 percent and defending his Olympic title.

His 2012 season started well as he won indoor titles in 60-meter hurdles. He qualified for the 2012 London Games but reinjured the same tendon on the first hurdle. He hopped the rest of the way to the finish, failing to medal.

THE FINAL RUN

The end for Liu came at the 2012 London Games when he reinjured his tendon on the first hurdle of his first race. He kissed the last hurdle before crossing the finish line on one leg. He was rolled off the track in a wheelchair. Although it was his last competitive race in the hurdles, Liu did not officially retire from racing until April 2015.

SUN YANG
CHINA SWIMMING

1,500-Meter Freestyle World Record at 2012 Games

There is no telling what the scene in Beijing would have been like if Chinese swimmer Sun Yang had peaked before the 2008 Summer Olympics. Sun Yang made his Olympic debut in his home country as a 16-year-old, but it was not until the next Games that he became a legend.

It was at the 2012 Athens Games that Sun won four Olympic medals—two gold, one silver, and one bronze. Sun won gold in the 400-meter freestyle with an Olympic record swim, which was actually the first gold medal ever won by a Chinese man in modern Olympics history.

Sun then set the world record in the 1,500-meter freestyle with a 14 minute, 34.14-second swim. His time was 3 seconds faster than any other time in history. Sun was the first swimmer to win Olympic gold in both the 400 and 1,500 since the boycotted 1980 Moscow Games. He also won silver in the 200-meter freestyle and a team bronze in the 4x200 freestyle relay in Athens.

Sun kept up his winning ways over the next four years,

PURE DOMINANCE

With his 2017 world championship in the 200-meter freestyle, Sun Yang became the first male swimmer in the world to ever win major international gold medals (Olympics and world championship) in all freestyle races between 200 and 1,500 meters. The 800-meter freestyle didn't exist for men in Olympic competition until the 2020 Tokyo Games.

winning multiple world championships and setting the table for another successful run in the next Olympics.

At the 2016 Rio Games, Sun won gold in the 200-meter freestyle and silver in the 400-meter freestyle. With the gold in the 200, Sun is the only swimmer to win Olympic gold in each of the 200-meter, 400-meter, and 1,500-meter events.

Sun is the most-decorated Chinese swimmer of all time between the Olympics and world championships.

DOPING SCANDAL

Sun faced a lifetime swimming ban after he interfered with an out-of-competition drug test by the World Anti-Doping Agency (WADA) in 2018. The International Swimming Federation did not sanction Sun for his actions, but WADA appealed for him to be banned. Doping accusations have dogged him throughout his career. He served a doping suspension in 2014.

KEVIN YOUNG
USA TRACK AND FIELD

400-Meter Hurdles World Record at 1992 Games

Kevin Young thought he might have something special in store before lining up for the finals of the 400-meter hurdles at the 1992 Barcelona Games. And did he ever.

Young ran the race of his life in front of 80,000 track enthusiasts at Olympic Stadium. He sprinted out to a blazing-fast start and then effortlessly glided around the track and over the 36-inch-high hurdles. Young took a big lead over his competitors in the first 300 meters, and he roared down the final stretch to take gold. He not only broke the world record with his time of 46.78 seconds; he obliterated it. All this was despite him clipping the final hurdle and appearing to ease up before the finish line.

"A lot of hard work and sacrifices, great coaching, a huge investment, and more than anything else, one hell of a race," Young recalled.

Young became the first person in history to break the 47-second barrier, and he ended the 16-year reign of countryman Edwin Moses as the world record holder.

Only two other runners have broken 47 seconds since Young did it, but his time set in 1992 still stands as the world record going into the 2020 Olympic trials for hurdlers around the world. It was the only Olympic medal for Young, whose first Olympics were at the 1988 Seoul Games.

Young won the world championship in the event the following year, but injuries plagued him throughout his career, and he was forced to retire. He was inducted into USA National Track & Field Hall of Fame in 2006.

A COLLEGE WALK-ON

Young went to David Starr Jordan High School in Los Angeles (Florence Griffith-Joyner's alma mater). Young was moderately successful in high school—finishing third in the 1984 state meet in the 110-meter hurdles—but he had to walk on to the UCLA team. In his sophomore year, he specialized in the 400-meter hurdles, and his career took off from there.

Kevin Young runs the race of his life at the 1992 Barcelona Games, shattering the world record that had stood for 29 years.

GAME CHANGING EVENTS

MELBOURNE, AUSTRALIA

Seven countries boycotted these games, including the Netherlands, Switzerland, and Spain. These three were protesting Soviet military action in Hungary, a conflict that played out in competition. The IOC allowed the Soviets to compete, and in water polo they played Hungary in a semifinal match that turned violent. "Blood in the Water" screamed the headlines. Hungary won and went on to claim gold.

LONDON, UK

After six years of World War II, the world looked to war-ravaged London to pull off the first Olympics since 1936 (Germany and Japan were banned). It was not easy. These were dubbed the Austerity Games in a London that was broke. No new stadiums were built, and food was rationed, but the Games themselves were a huge success.

MUNICH, GERMAN

The 1972 Munich Games were marre attack on the Olympic Village. Pale terrorists killed two Israeli athletes a nine others hostage. The drama pla on live television around the w botched rescue attempt 20 hours la all nine Israeli hostages and five terrorists dead.

POLITICS...CRISIS...SOCIAL CHANGE

OR USE BY WHITE PERSONS
HESE PUBLIC PREMISES AND THE AMENITIES
HEREOF HAVE BEEN RESERVED FOR THE
XCLUSIVE USE OF WHITE PERSONS.
By Order   Provincial Secretary

R GEBRUIK DEUR BLANKES
HIERDIE OPENBARE PERSEEL EN DIE GERIEWE
DAARVAN IS VIR DIE UITSLUITLIKE GEBRUIK
VAN BLANKES AANGEWYS.
Op Las Provinsiale Sekretaris

MOSCOW, USSR

In December of 1979, Soviet troops attacked the Afghan capital of Kabul, executed president Hafizullah Amin and made Babrak Karmal, who was a Soviet supporter, the new leader. This kicked off what would become a 10-year occupation. The United States led the idea of boycotting the Games if the Soviets did not withdraw, and ultimately more than 60 countries decided not to send athletes to Moscow.

MONTREAL, CANADA

ty-two African nations boycotted 1976 Montreal Games at the last te when the IOC allowed New nd to participate after having sent gby team to play in South Africa. South African government was subject of international scorn and tions due to its policy of racial egation called apartheid.

RIO DE JANEIRO, BRAZIL

The IOC allowed 10 athletes without a country to participate under the Olympic flag. Amidst a worldwide refugee crisis, the IOC funded the training for the selected athletes. Examples of what they had survived include the Syrian Civil War and tribal genocide in the Democratic Republic of the Congo.

RESEARCH PROJECTS

Major moments on the world stage have impacted the Olympics through the years. The Research Projects below will bring a deeper perspective to these moments and the events that shaped them.

1. Who was the terrorist group that murdered the Israeli team members during the 1972 Games? Four terrorists survived the Munich Massacre. Make a chart with a row for each terrorist, and fill in columns indicating the sentence they received, how they were released, where they went after being freed, and what ultimately became of them.

2. The 2016 Rio Games featured the Refugee Olympic Team. What does it mean to be a refugee? How is it different from being an immigrant? How does someone become a refugee in the U.S.?

3. The South African policy of apartheid was the reason for a large boycott of the 1976 Montreal Games. What was apartheid and who were the significant figures in its history? Prepare synopsis biographies of at least three major personalities.

4. Switzerland, Spain, and the Netherlands boycotted the 1956 Melbourne Games to protest the Soviet invasion of Hungary. Four other countries also boycotted these games. Look up which ones those were, and why they boycotted. Present the information in a chart.

5. At the 1948 Summer Olympics in London, the former British colonies of India and Pakistan competed as independent nations for the first time. So did the Philippines. Which country did the Philippines gain independence from? Write a brief synopsis on how each of these three countries came to be.

OLYMPIC GLOSSARY OF KEY TERMS

archery—the sport of shooting arrows with a bow.

banned—to prohibit, especially by legal means.

compete—to strive consciously or unconsciously for an objective (such as position, profit, or a prize).

decathlon—an athletic contest consisting of ten different track and field events.

doping—the use of a substance (such as an anabolic steroid or erythropoietin) or technique (such as blood doping) to illegally improve athletic performance.

equestrian—of, relating to, or featuring horseback riding.

heat—one of several preliminary contests held to eliminate less competent contenders.

host city—the city that is selected to be the primary location for Olympic ceremonies and events.

hurdle—a light barrier that competitors must leap over in races.

medal—a piece of metal often resembling a coin and having a stamped design that is issued to commemorate a person or event or awarded for excellence or achievement; may also mean to win a medal.

nationality—a legal relationship involving allegiance on the part of an individual and usually protection on the part of the state.

opponent—a contestant that you are matched against.

participant—a person who takes part in something.

preliminary—a minor match preceding the main event.

pommel horse—a gymnastics apparatus for swinging and balancing feats that consists of a padded rectangular or cylindrical form with two handgrips called pommels on the top and that is supported in a horizontal position above the floor.

qualify—meet the required standard.

referee—the official in a sport who is expected to ensure fair play.

repechage—a race (especially in rowing) in which runners-up in the eliminating heats compete for a place in the final race.

spectator—one who looks on or watches.

sportsmanship—fairness, honesty, and courtesy in following the rules of a game.

stamina—enduring strength and energy.

standings—an ordered listing of scores or results showing the relative positions of competitors (individuals or teams) in an event.

substitute—a player or competitor that takes the place of another.

torch—a cylindrical or cone-shaped object in which the Olympic flame is ceremonially carried.

vault—to execute a leap using the hands or a pole.

venue—the place where any event or action is held.

victory—a successful ending of a struggle or contest; a win.

EDUCATIONAL VIDEO LINKS

Usain Bolt: http://x-qr.net/1Jte
Dick Fosbury: http://x-qr.net/1Jhx
Florence Griffith-Joyner: http://x-qr.net/1M58
Michael Johnson: http://x-qr.net/1Jz8
Jackie Joyner-Kersee: http://x-qr.net/1LyT
Katie Ledecky: http://x-qr.net/1JuC
Carl Lewis: http://x-qr.net/1Kw8
Greg Louganis: http://x-qr.net/1J2g
Jenny Thompson: http://x-qr.net/1JyD
Kevin Young: http://x-qr.net/1Kes
Kerri Walsh Jennings & Misty May-Treanor: http://x-qr.net/1LDX

FURTHER READING

Aim, Ellen. *Misty May/Kerri Walsh: Dynamic Duo: SportStars Volume 6.* Creative Media Publishing, 2016.

Lohn, John. *The 100 Greatest Swimmers in History (Swimming).* Lanham, MD: Rowman & Littlefield Publishers, 2018.

Phelps, Michael. *Beneath the Surface: My Story.* New York, NY: Sports Publishing, 2016.

INTERNET RESOURCES

https://www.olympic.org/sports
The website for the International Olympic Committee (IOC). Acting as a catalyst for collaboration between all parties of the Olympic family, from the National Olympic Committees (NOCs), the International Sports Federations (IFs), the athletes, the Organizing Committees for the Olympic Games (OCOGs), to The Olympic Partners (TOP), broadcast partners, and United Nations agencies, the International Olympic Committee shepherds success through a wide range of programs and projects.

https://www.britannica.com/sports/Olympic-Games
Encyclopedia Britannica's page detailing the Olympic Games, from ancient Greece through the upcoming Games in Tokyo, Japan, in 2020. Visitors will learn about the history of the Games, Women and the Olympic Games, the International Olympic Committee who runs the Games, and much more.

https://www.iaaf.org/records/by-category/olympic-games-records
The Olympic Games records by category on the International Association of Athletics Federation website. The IAAF is the international governing body for the sport of athletics. It was founded in 1912 as the International Amateur Athletic Federation. It is currently headquartered in Monaco.

INDEX

PHOTO CREDITS

AUTHOR BIOGRAPHY

SCOTT MCDONALD was a high school athlete in West Monroe, Louisiana, before serving 4 years in the U.S. Navy as a gunner's mate. He began his writing career at Richland College in Dallas, Texas, and went on to the University of Texas at Austin, where he majored in journalism. McDonald covered sports for high school and small colleges at *The Dallas Morning News*. He served as the managing editor of a newspaper near Austin and as publisher at another newspaper in Texas. He has covered sports for 20 years and he has covered Olympians and Paralympians since 2009. The Texas High School Coaches Association named him the State Sportswriter of the Year in 2014.